fuzzbuzz

Teacher's Resource Book

Word learning and phonics

Colin Harris

Oxford University Press

1996

Teacher's notes

The materials contained within this book are designed to make the learning processes demanded by Level 2 of the *fuzzbuzz* scheme as thorough, and as enjoyable, as possible. The materials are designed to be used in conjunction with *words 2*, *fuzzbuzz words box 2* and the two phonic workbooks (*letters 1* and *Letters 2*).

Most of the ideas for apparatus which are outlined in Chapters 8 and 9 of the *fuzzbuzz Teacher's Book* are included, but teachers will note that many of the word-learning games incorporated in the Level 1 *Teacher's Resource Book* have not been included. Children working at Level 2 are expected to learn words with less help.

Much more emphasis has been placed on giving help with the phonic programme. This has been organised to fit exactly with the phonic sequence presented in the two workbooks (*letters 1* and the revised version of *Letters 2* to be published shortly. The material also corresponds to the original *Letters 2* but is in a somewhat different arrangement). The emphasis has been placed on the first five phonic units which contain all the basic work. An extra workbook - *More words and letters* - gives support for Phonic unit 6 which concentrates on words of more than one syllable.

In this resource book a lot of space has been devoted to the 'notched cards', which in the author's opinion are by far the best method of teaching consonant-vowel and consonant-consonant blends. As in all the other *fuzzbuzz* materials, these cards are presented in a highly-structured, step-by-step sequence. Teachers are strongly recommended to try them out.

The final section of this book addresses the problem of recording and assessment, and provides some useful record forms which are linked directly to the *fuzzbuzz* materials.

Oxford University Press, Great Clarendon Street, Oxford OX2 6DP

Oxford New York
Athens Auckland Bangkok Bogota Buenos Aires
Bombay Calcutta Cape Town Dar es Salaam
Delhi Florence Hong Kong Istanbul Karachi
Kuala Lumpur Madras Madrid Melbourne Mexico City
Nairobi Paris Singapore Taipei Tokyo Toronto

and associated companies in
Berlin Ibadan

Oxford is a trade mark of Oxford University Press

© Oxford University Press 1996
Illustrated by Jane Bottomley

ISBN 0 19 838193 X

Printed in Great Britain

Contents

About this book: a quick overview

The posters

8

Black Angus has a big, black stick.

22

The posters present all the characters (e.g. the clan, the grinlings, the Honkbonk) and the main locations (e.g. the glen, Zaxon) which appear in the various Level 2 stories.

In this level, each poster is labelled with a short, conventionally-punctuated sentence, to introduce the idea that sentences begin with a capital letter and end with a full stop.

The tiny numerals in the bottom left-hand corner of each poster indicate the book number in which that character or location first occurs.

The posters are intended for general display and discussion.

4

The individual word cards

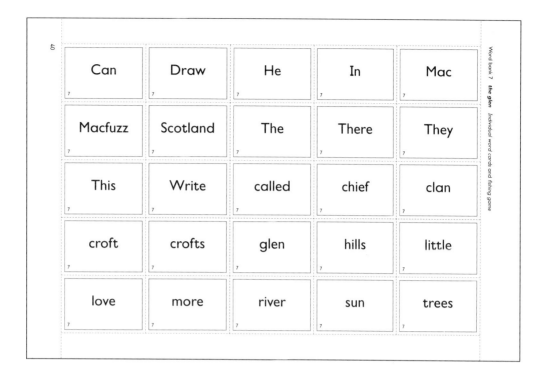

These have been designed to complement the large flashcards which are already available as part of the *fuzzbuzz* scheme. They present the six banks of twenty-five words which are used in the core books of Level 2 (books 7–12). The numerals in the bottom left-hand corner of each card indicate to which bank that particular word belongs. The word banks are intended to be cut out and given to individual pupils to keep, to take home, to learn, or to revise. They may or may not be mounted on card.

In addition, individual word cards have been included for the new words which are introduced in the *fuzzbuzz facts* books. They are designed to be used in conjunction with the *Words for fuzzbuzz facts* workbook which accompanies that series. Again, each card bears a small letter and/or numeral in the bottom left-hand corner in order to identify the book to which it relates:

Letter / Numeral	Key
F	These words appear in all six fact books
F1	These words are for *Animals in the house*
F2	These words are for *Animals on the farm*
F3	These words are for *Animals in the garden*
F4	These words are for *Sea-shore animals*
F5	These words are for *Animals on the dump*
F6	These words are for *Pond animals*

Phonic work

The supplementary phonic work contained within this resource book, is designed to parallel the six phonic units presented in the two phonic workbooks which accompany Level 2 of the *fuzzbuzz* scheme (*letters 1* and *Letters 2*). Basically, the six phonic units cover the following work:

Phonic unit	Work covered	
1	The letter sounds: **a b e g m t u**	(*letters 1*, pp. 3–21)
2	The letter sounds: **c d h j o r s v**	(*letters 1*, pp. 22–41)
3	The letter sounds: **f k l n p w y z** Recognition of capital letters for above.	(*letters 1*, pp. 42–64)
4	The letter sound: **x** The letter combinations: **ch ck qu sh st th ing**	(*Letters 2*, pp. 3–25)
5	Initial and final blends Final double letters	(*Letters 2*, pp. 26–49)
6	Using all the above skills to read words of more than one syllable.	(*Letters 2*, pp. 50–64)

Each piece of apparatus is clearly numbered (1, 2, 3, 4, 5, or 6) so that it is easy to tell which phonic unit it supports. Where there is a sequence of cards within a given phonic unit, two numbers are given, for example: (1/2)

In this case the first number refers to the phonic unit, the second number refers to where in the sequence that card belongs, so card 1/2 is the second card in a particular sequence which supports Phonic unit 1.

Notched cards

These provide an activity for two children or for a child and an adult. In Level 1 the notched cards are used to teach whole words; in Level 2 they are used to teach the various letter combinations and blends (consonant-vowel/consonant-consonant/consonant-consonant-vowel).

The cards are presented in A4 format. On one side of the card are the illustrations, on the other side are the blends. A series of arrow-shaped notches, cut into the edges of the card, point to the blends or to the pictures depending on which side of the card you are viewing. One child holds the card upright, facing the pictures. He or she chooses a picture randomly and says aloud the whole word which that picture represents (e.g. tap, magnet, gun, and so on). The child sitting opposite must then work out how that particular word begins and place a finger, or a pencil, into the notch alongside that specific blend.

A quick glance will show that several words on each card share the same initial letter. The children are therefore unable to predict the correct answer by looking at the first letter alone; they must also take the second letter into account.

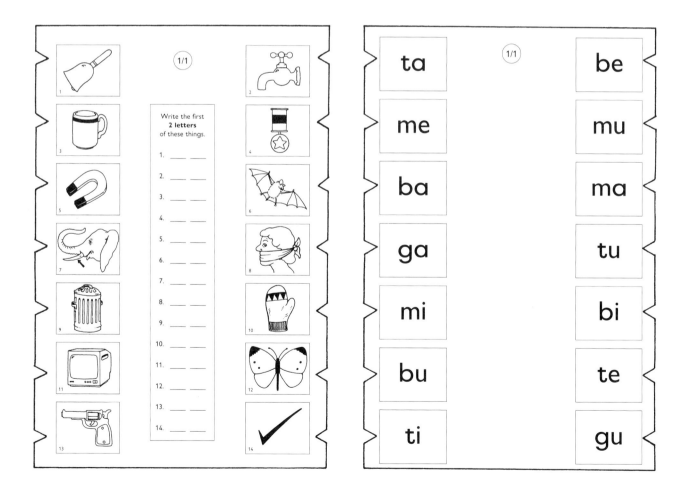

Phonic worksheets

The picture sides of the notched cards can be used as stand-alone
phonic worksheets. On each sheet the pictures are numbered 1-14,
and a central panel is provided for the child to write in the relevant
letters for each illustration.

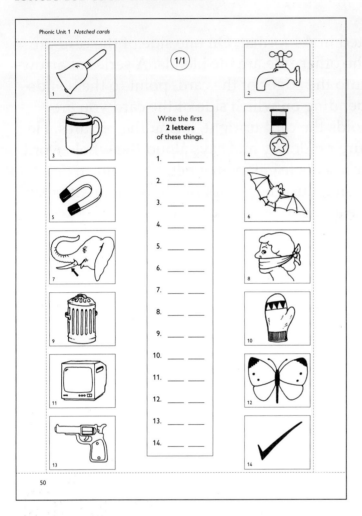

Individual letter cards

These are sheets of individual letters, numbered according to the
phonic unit in which they first appear.

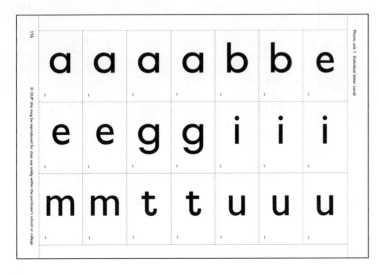

From the teacher's point of view, the letter cards are especially useful as they are printed in exactly the same font as the *fuzzbuzz* books.

They are intended to be cut out and used in word-building exercises. They can be used face-upwards on the pupil's desk or table top, or they can be mounted on differently-shaped pieces of card and used in the following ways:

separate letters stuck onto long strips of card

These cards can be placed in a wooden or perspex container which has a long pocket.

separate letters stuck onto folded cards

These cards can be hung along a thin rail made from a simple wooden frame and thin doweling.

The fishing game

This is a game for one to several players.

The twenty-five words from each bank are put on to twenty-five fish, and a metal paper clip attached to each fish's mouth.
The fish are then put into a bowl, a tin, or onto a piece of blue paper/cloth which represents a pond. The child is then provided with a simple 'fishing rod', but on the end of the line is a magnet, not a hook.

The child then 'catches' the fish by attracting the paper clips to the magnet. If he can read the word, he keeps the fish. If not, he must put it back.

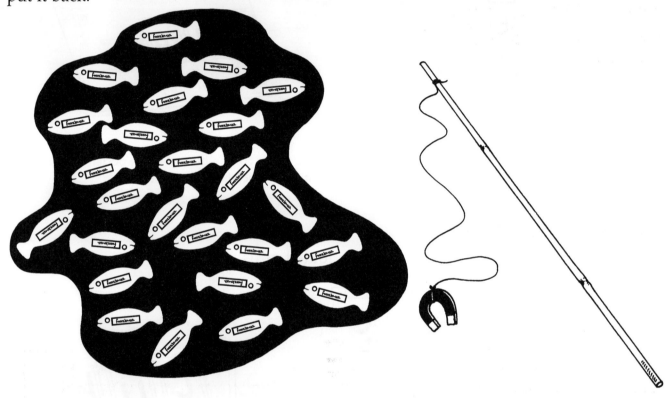

pond cut out of paper or cloth

fishing rod made from cane, string, and magnet

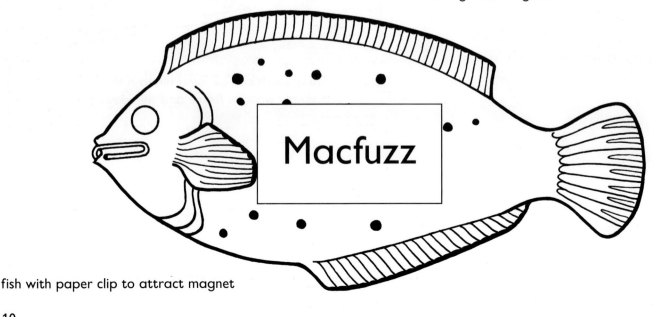

Macfuzz

fish with paper clip to attract magnet

Phonic word lists

These are simple lists of words which can be built up from the letter sounds introduced in the first five phonic units. Once again, they will be particularly useful because they are printed in the correct *fuzzbuzz* font.

These lists can be photocopied, enlarged, or reduced, and cut out to form the basis of a variety of games and apparatus of the teacher's own design or choosing.

They can also be used to provide words for the croft word-wheel.

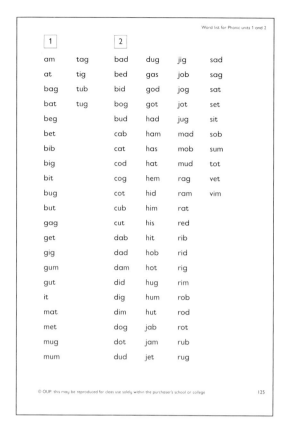

Word list for Phonic units 1 and 2

1		2			
am	tag	bad	dug	jig	sad
at	tig	bed	gas	job	sag
bag	tub	bid	god	jog	sat
bat	tug	bog	got	jot	set
beg		bud	had	jug	sit
bet		cab	ham	mad	sob
bib		cat	has	mob	sum
big		cod	hat	mud	tot
bit		cog	hem	rag	vet
bug		cot	hid	ram	vim
but		cub	him	rat	
gag		cut	his	red	
get		dab	hit	rib	
gig		dad	hob	rid	
gum		dam	hot	rig	
gut		did	hug	rim	
it		dig	hum	rob	
mat		dim	hut	rod	
met		dog	jab	rot	
mug		dot	jam	rub	
mum		dud	jet	rug	

© OUP this may be reproduced for class use solely within the purchaser's school or college   125

The croft word-wheel

This is simply a device for presenting whole words from the various phonic units. As the wheel is turned at the top of the croft, the words appear one after the other in the left-hand window.

The number on the front door indicates which phonic unit is being used. This piece of apparatus can also be adapted for use as a sight-learning aid for the various word banks linked to the storybooks.

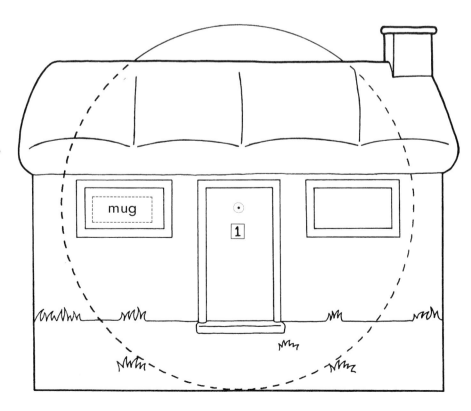

mug

1

Rewards

The word 'good' is introduced very early in the *fuzzbuzz* scheme (in the second bank of sight words) to enable the teacher to write a favourable comment, *which the child can actually read*, next to praiseworthy work. During the course of Level 2, a variety of readable comments can be used:

Comment	When it becomes readable
This is good.	After storybook 7 (*The glen*)
Very good!	After storybook 9 (*The haggis hunt*)
Tip-top!	After Phonic unit 3
Smashing!	After Phonic unit 4
Splendid!	After Phonic unit 5 and during Phonic unit 6
Fantastic!	After Phonic unit 5 and during Phonic unit 6
Brilliant!	After Phonic unit 5 and during Phonic unit 6

These comments are included in the resource book as a series of stamps which can be cut out and stuck down next to work which shows particular excellence or effort:

It is a sad fact that many children who experience reading difficulties may also fail to excel in many areas (often due to lack of confidence rather than anything else). These children are often at the end of the line when awards and certificates are being handed out.

For this reason, also included in the resource book is a photocopiable certificate, which can be awarded to all those children who have successfully completed the work of Level 2. It can be given immediately after the children pass the end-of-level tests which are described below.

Wherever possible, these certificates should be given added value by being presented at a special occasion such as a school assembly. This can do wonders for individual self-confidence and increased motivation.

Recording progress

Day-to-day recording

The Daily Record Sheet comprises the full sequence of work from Level 2, (excluding the *fuzzbuzz facts* sequence of books) presented on a single, A4 sheet:

fuzzbuzz Level 2							

DAILY RECORD SHEET

Name		**Date** Level 2 started			
		Date Level 2 completed			

CORE BOOKS	Sequence of work	Started			Finished			Comments
		d	m	y	d	m	y	
	Word bank 7: 25 words (*words 2* pp. 3-9)							
	Book 7: *The glen*							
	Phonic unit 1: (*letters 1* pp. 3-21)							
	Word bank 8: 25 words (*words 2* pp. 10-17)							
	Book 8: *The clan*							
	Phonic unit 2: (*letters 1* pp. 22-41)							
	Wordbank 9: 25 words (*words 2* pp. 18-23)							
	Book 9: *The haggis hunt*							
	Phonic unit 3: (*letters 1* pp.42-64)							
	Word bank 10: 25 words (*words 2* pp. 24-29)							
	Book 10: *Jock the pocket*							
	Phonic unit 4: (*Letters* pp. 3-25)							
	W... ...ords 2 ...35)							

Although it will not always be required on a strictly daily basis, this sheet should be routinely dated whenever a pupil starts or finishes a new word bank, phonic unit, or storybook. The pupils should be fully involved in this process and, before long, the children themselves will remind you whenever it is time to make an entry on the sheet, making your job much easier. Properly completed, the sheet will enable you to check on individual progress over a period of time. The information it contains will enable you to look at each child's rate of learning. Is he or she making steady progress, or speeding up? If you feel that a pupil is slowing down, you will have the information to hand to check on this, and you will be able to tell whether a particular section of work is causing problems.

Regular recording also provides another positive factor in the motivation of the children; as more and more dates are entered and their charts begin to fill up, they can actually see that they are making progress. Finally, as this sheet contains all the work of Level 2 in the correct sequence (including an indication of page numbers where appropriate) it will eliminate any confusion about what each child should move on to next. It is also extremely useful for informing new or temporary teachers about exactly where the child is, and where he or she is going, thus ensuring much-needed continuity.

Testing

Some teachers may wish to test a child before he or she begins working on Level 2, in order to establish a base line to provide a fair comparison later; two children may start on Level 2 at the same time, but one of them may already know a substantial scatter of the work to be introduced, whereas the other may know none at all. Nearly all teachers will wish to test the children when they have completed the work of Level 2, either when they have finished the core books or when they have finished all or part of the extension work, in order to establish whether or not they are ready to begin the work of Level 3. The following tests can be used to meet all these needs.

There are four separate tests: **Test 1** examines the child's ability to read a sample of the irregular words which are introduced during the course of both Levels 1 and 2; **Test 2** examines the child's ability to recognise lower and upper case letters and to identify them by sound; **Test 3** examines the child's ability to use the letter sounds to build up three-letter words, words with initial and final blends, and digraphs and words of more than one syllable; and **Test 4**, presents all the above skills in a single passage of continuous text, followed by a series of written questions which require written answers.

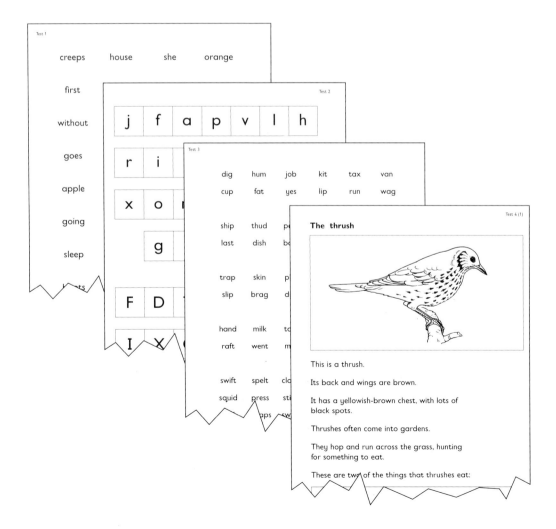

Test 1

creeps   house   she   orange

first

without

goes

apple

going

sleep

Test 2

| j | f | a | p | v | l | h |

| r | i |

| x | o |

| g |

| F | D |

| I | X |

Test 3

dig   hum   job   kit   tax   van
cup   fat   yes   lip   run   wag

ship   thud   p
last   dish   b

trap   skin   p
slip   brag   d

hand   milk   t
raft   went   m

swift   spelt   cl
squid   press   sti

Test 4 (1)

The thrush

This is a thrush.

Its back and wings are brown.

It has a yellowish-brown chest, with lots of black spots.

Thrushes often come into gardens.

They hop and run across the grass, hunting for something to eat.

These are two of the things that thrushes eat:

Each test has an accompanying record sheet which is designed to be used on an individual basis. Each record form has a box for the pupil's name and spaces for at least three dates for those teachers who may need to administer the test more than once. If this is the case, it is a good idea to use a different coloured pen on each occasion, and to write the date in the specific colour being used. It will then be much easier to check at a later date which performance was which.

As the child reads from the test sheet, the teacher can follow on the record sheet. Correct responses should be marked with a small tick, mistakes should be written in where they occur, giving the actual response which the child makes. If a child simply does not know a particular word, or makes no response, the letter N should be written above the word:

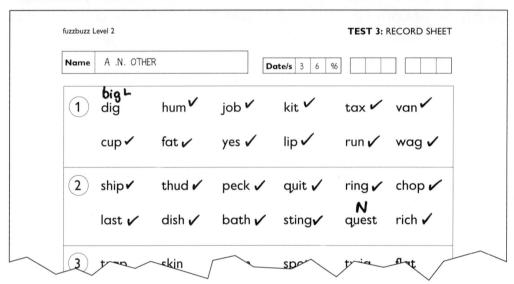

The final page in the series of test and record sheets is a **summary sheet**. This will show at a glance exactly how well the child has performed in all the tests.

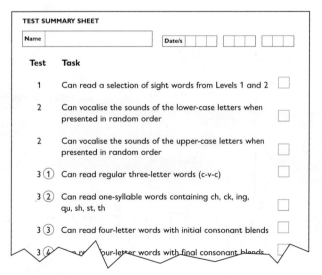

Children who pass the various tests with around 95% accuracy, should be ready to go on to Level 3 of the *fuzzbuzz* scheme.

7

This is Scotland.

7

This glen is in Scotland.

7

There is a croft in the glen.

A clan lives in the glen.

7

This is Macfuzz the buzz.

8

Black Angus has a big, black stick.

8

Windbag has some bagpipes.

8

This is Jock the pocket.

8

Tosh has big boots.

8

This is Hilda Macfuzz.

8

Big Ben has a red vest.

8

This is Don the bonnet.

12.3

The slinx travels in this rocket.

This is Zaxon.

12.4

These grinlings live on Zaxon.

12.5

This is the Honkbonk.

Making the apparatus

Photocopying

It is worth reading the manual which comes with the photocopier to see if it contains any useful tips and hints. You should certainly check to see if the lighter/darker or contrast buttons are set correctly.

The quality of photocopying paper you use will also affect the final result, so it is worth keeping a reserve of good quality paper for those special jobs. Always keep this paper in damp-proof conditions - damp paper often jams in the works. And when loading a new batch of paper, riffle it so the sheets separate slightly before blocking it back together - this will also help to prevent jams.

As a general rule, it is always a good idea to clean the glass plate on which you lay the materials to be photocopied. It is almost certain that the previous user has left behind smudges of ink or correction fluid, which will show up on your copies.

If you spot a recurring mark, which is always in the same place on your copies, a quick clean of the glass should eradicate it. If there is a recurring mark which changes position on subsequent copies, the fault will lie on the drum inside the machine and the engineer should be called. (In fact, it is always a good idea to do all your important photocopying straight after the machine has been serviced.)

The equipment you will need

Once the relevant sheets have been photocopied, all the apparatus can be made with a basic minimum of equipment. You will need the following:

> a pencil,
> a rubber,
> a ruler,
> a good pair of scissors and/or a rotary cutter
> some adhesive (the sort that is packaged in a pop-up tube, like
>   lipstick, is the easiest to use. PVA adhesive or wallpaper
>   paste can be used for large areas.).

Also useful is a metal scoring ruler, and a slim modelling knife with interchangeable blades (like a scalpel), which is extremely handy for lifting and positioning small pieces of paper once adhesive has been applied to them.

Using card

Most of the apparatus has been designed to be mounted on card. Even the posters will last longer if they are stuck down onto card first. The longevity of your equipment will depend on the quality of card used, therefore it is recommended that you use six-sheet card for all the mounting work. This is strong enough to last for a long time, yet is not too thick to cut, score, or bend.

Plastic Covering

Your apparatus will last much longer if it is covered in transparent plastic. This can be obtained in rolls from most educational suppliers. If you have access to a laminating machine, so much the better. If you are going to colour some of the illustrations on the posters or apparatus, a plastic covering will enhance and 'lift' the colours beautifully.

When using one of the proprietary transparent plastic rolls, remember that it is best to spread the plastic film sticky side up on a flat surface and then position your card on to it. If you are covering both sides of a piece of card with plastic, try to make sure that the film covering both the front and the back surfaces is slightly larger than the card itself. Now trim the edges a couple of millimetres away from the edge of the card, leaving the card completely encapsulated. This will prevent the plastic from peeling away later.

The templates

Templates have been provided to help you to mark out the notched cards, make the fish for the fishing game, and to create the word wheels.

The notched cards

Photocopy the pairs of pages for each phonic unit required and trim along the lines indicated. You will need an A4 sheet of work card for every pair copied.

Use **Template 1** to make a ruler you can draw round. Using this ruler, mark out the notches on *both* the long edges of your work card.

To save marking out the reverse of your card, cut out the notches first and then stick down the photocopied pages on to opposite sides (the same way up) so that the notches point to the centres of the squares.

The fishing game

Use **Template 2** to produce the number of fish you require (usually twenty-five).

Next, photocopy and cut out a set of the individual word cards. These cards will fit inside the boxes already drawn on the fish. Slot a medium-sized paper clip onto the mouth of each fish (see the illustration on page 10). The eye on each fish is an ideal place to print in the word bank number. Now all you have to make is a rod with a magnet and the pond. (A plastic fish tank provides another alternative.)

The word wheels

Photocopy the croft (**Template 3**) and stick it onto card. Cut it out and cut out the dotted rectangle in the left hand window. Photocopy one of the circular wheels (**Template 4**). Write, or stick down, the selection of words you wish to use in the series of boxes. Save one box to write in the number of the phonic unit to which the words belong (this may save confusion later on).

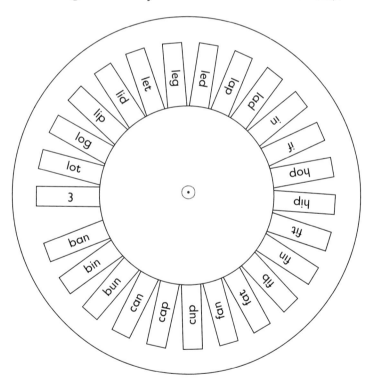

It is a good idea to photocopy the completed wheel and keep your original so you do not have to do all this work again if the finished piece of apparatus is damaged or lost. Stick the photocopy onto card, and cut it out when it is dry. Insert a brass paper fastener through the dotted circle on the croft door, then through the centre of the word wheel. Make sure the wheel spins freely, then press down the 'legs' on the paper fastener. Print the phonic unit number on the door itself. Your piece of apparatus is now ready to use.

Template 1

Notched cards

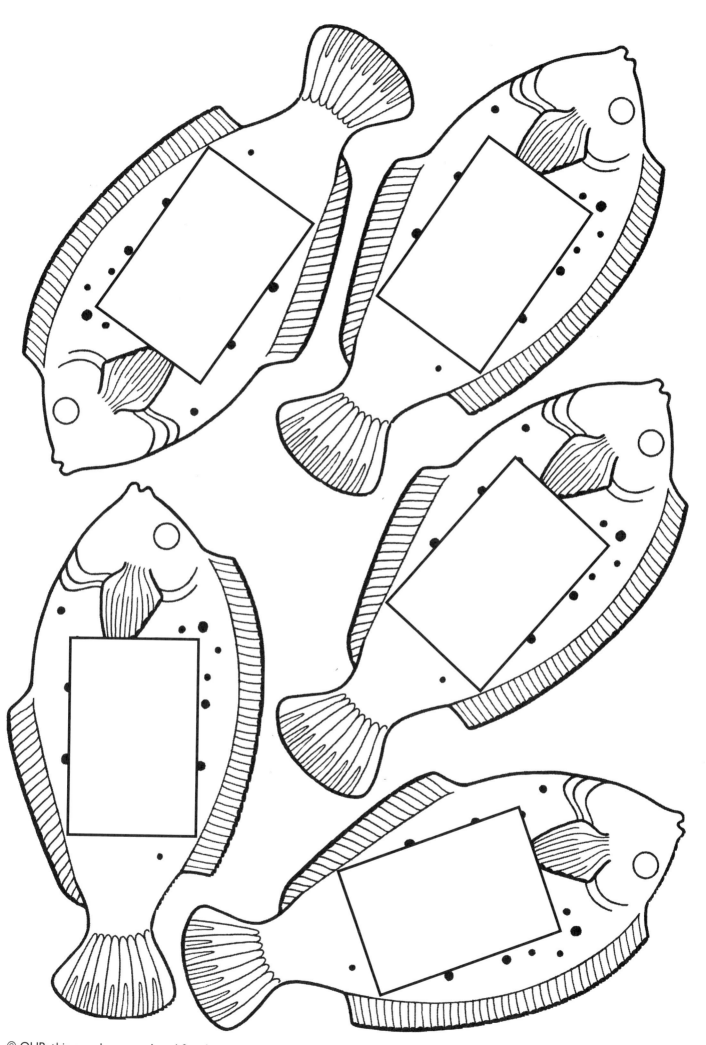

Template 3

Croft

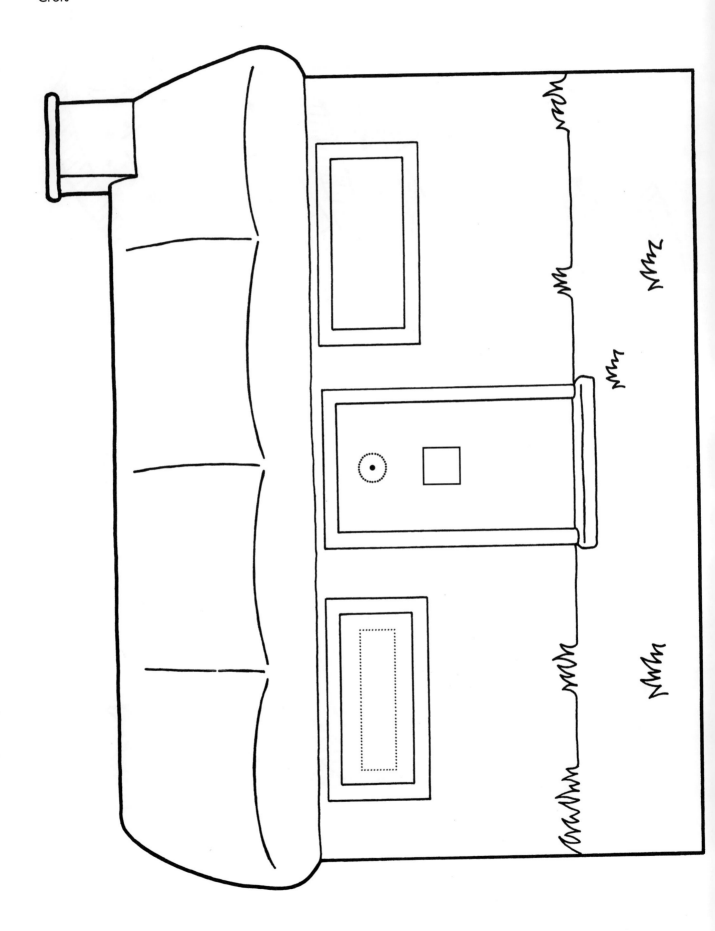

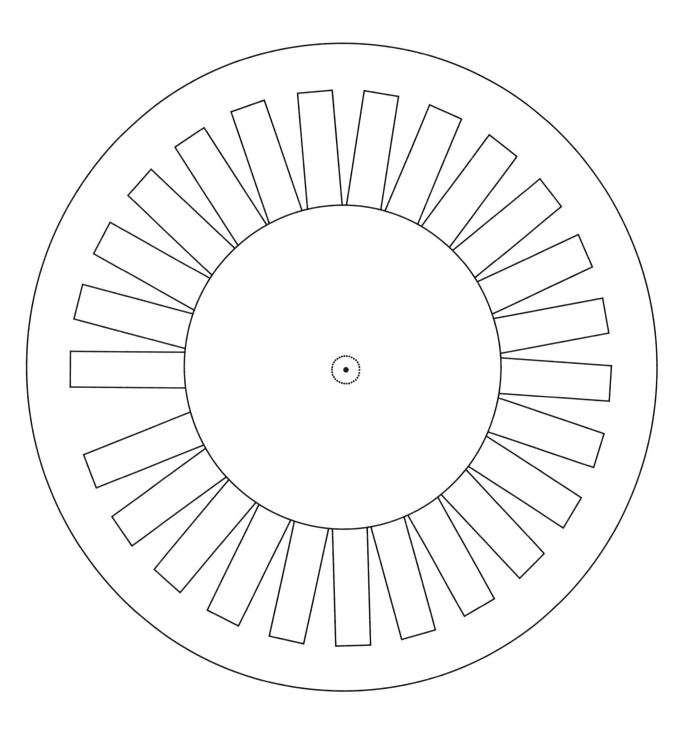

Mac	They	clan	little	trees
In	There	chief	hills	sun
He	The	called	glen	river
Draw	Scotland	Write	crofts	more
Can	Macfuzz	This	croft	love

Don	Windbag	grumpy	pocket	zip
Black	Tosh	cap	net	vest
Big	Jock	boots	last	stick
Ben	His	bonnet	kilt	so
Angus	Hilda	bagpipes	has	pom-pom

as	for	hunt	something	very
across	fast	have	ready	two
Where	dinner	haggis	off	top
It	cannot	gun	not	that
Down	because	grass	missing	still

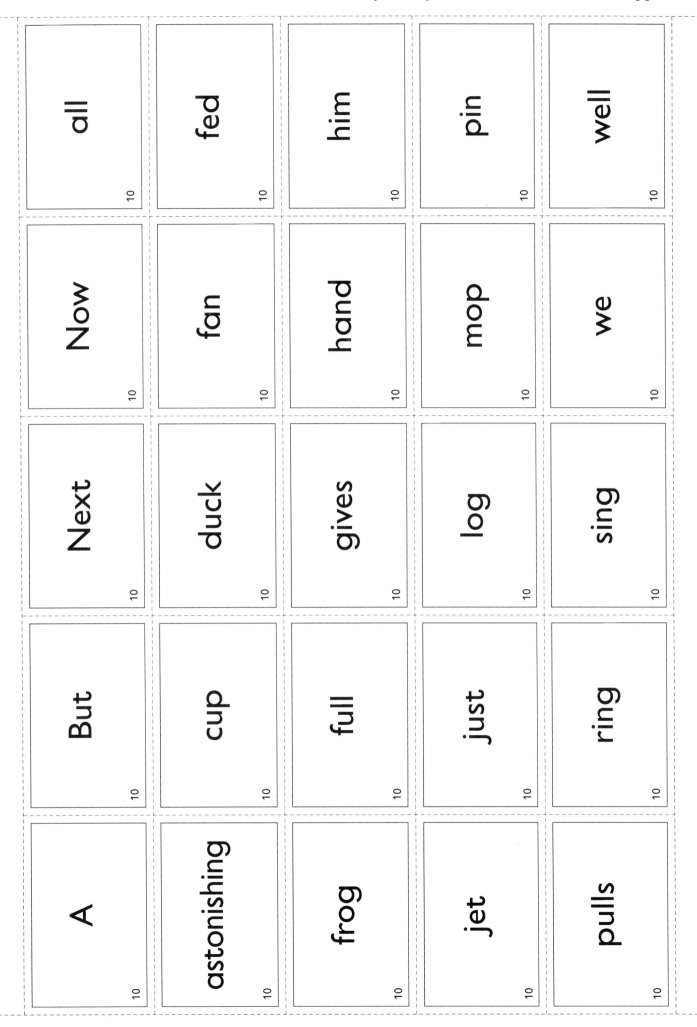

all	fed	him	pin	well
Now	fan	hand	mop	we
Next	duck	gives	log	sing
But	cup	full	just	ring
A	astonishing	frog	jet	pulls

Why	getting	kick	tells	will
What	fix	hits	sits	why
She	does	himself	she	trunk
Little	bank	her	pond	trips
At	asks	help	mud	trip

Some	crossbar	medal	summer	without
12	12	12	12	12
How	crashing	hot	slippery	win
12	12	12	12	12
Every	contest	ends	shock	wet
12	12	12	12	12
Crack	but	eat	runs	thick
12	12	12	12	12
All	Splash	do	one	tent
12	12	12	12	12

book	body	bird	baby	about
fly	female	eye	day	build
introduction	head	grow	four	food
male	look	long	like	lay
stay	page	night	mouth	many

week	your	mouse	babies
		F1	F1
time	year	martin	sound
three	winter	hibernate	protected
tail	which	flies	pupa
table	when	five	pipistrelle

caterpillar *F2*	cabbage *F2*	butterfly *F2*	burrow *F2*	barn *F2*
white *F2*	pupa *F2*	owl *F2*	mole *F2*	farm *F2*
				worm *F2*
part *F4*	larva *F4*	five *F4*	claws *F4*	blenny *F4*
teeth *F4*	star *F4*	shore *F4*	sea *F4*	pool *F4*

pincers F3	caterpillar F5	nettle F5	hibernate F6	
hibernate F3	butter F5	leaf F5	dangerous F6	water F6
hedge F3	spine F3	ground F5	boat F6	tadpole F6
ear F3	spider F3	fur F5	air F6	stickleback F6
ball F3	round F3	flies F5	pupa F5	snake F6

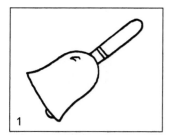

1

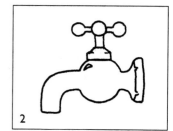

2

3

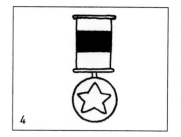

4

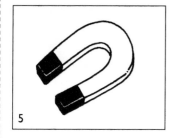

5

6

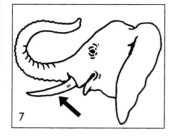

7

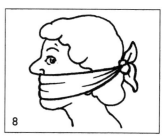

8

9

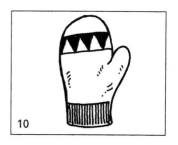

10

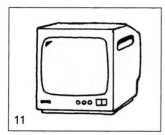

11

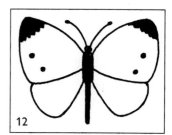

12

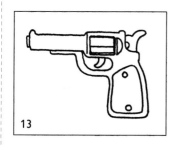

13

14

1/1

Write the first **2 letters** of these things.

1. ___ ___

2. ___ ___

3. ___ ___

4. ___ ___

5. ___ ___

6. ___ ___

7. ___ ___

8. ___ ___

9. ___ ___

10. ___ ___

11. ___ ___

12. ___ ___

13. ___ ___

14. ___ ___

ta	be
me	mu
ba	ma
ga	tu
mi	bi
bu	te
ti	gu

1/1

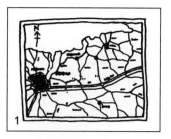

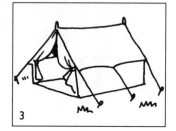

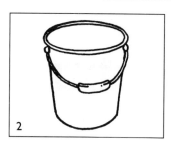

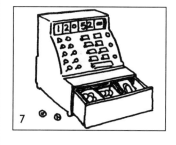

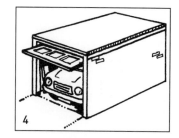

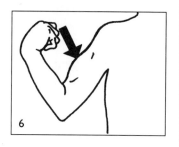

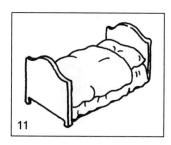

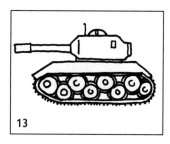

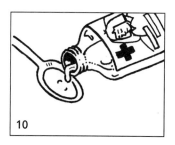

(1/2)

Write the first
2 letters
of these things.

1. ___ ___

2. ___ ___

3. ___ ___

4. ___ ___

5. ___ ___

6. ___ ___

7. ___ ___

8. ___ ___

9. ___ ___

10. ___ ___

11. ___ ___

12. ___ ___

13. ___ ___

14. ___ ___

bu	(1/2)	ma
ga		te
mu		bi
ba		ti
me		mi
tu		be
gu		ta

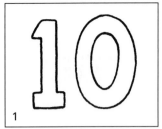

1

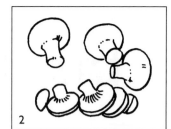

2

3

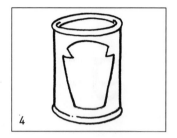

4

5

6

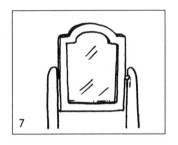

7

8

9

10

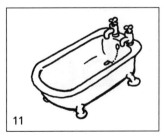

11

12

13

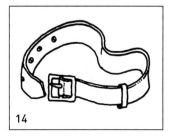

14

1/3

Write the first **2 letters** of these things.

1. ___ ___

2. ___ ___

3. ___ ___

4. ___ ___

5. ___ ___

6. ___ ___

7. ___ ___

8. ___ ___

9. ___ ___

10. ___ ___

11. ___ ___

12. ___ ___

13. ___ ___

14. ___ ___

mu	te
ti	ma
ga	bu
bi	mi
me	tu
ta	ba
be	gu

(1/3)

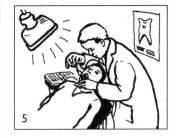

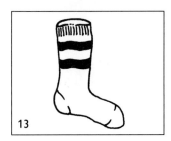

2/1

Write the first **2 letters** of these things.

1. ___ ___

2. ___ ___

3. ___ ___

4. ___ ___

5. ___ ___

6. ___ ___

7. ___ ___

8. ___ ___

9. ___ ___

10. ___ ___

11. ___ ___

12. ___ ___

13. ___ ___

14. ___ ___

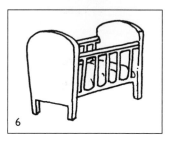

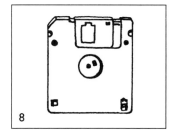

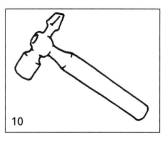

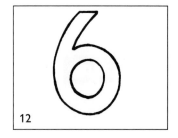

hu

ca

(2/1)

da

hi

co

de

di

ho

ha

cu

si

do

du

so

1

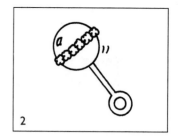

2

3

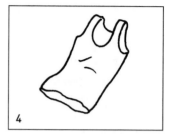

4

5

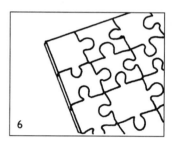

6

7

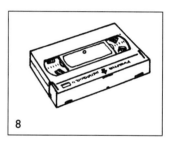

8

9

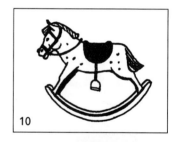

10

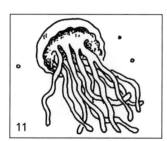

11

12

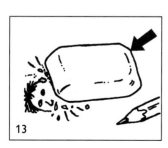

13

14

(2/2)

Write the first
2 letters
of these things.

1. ___ ___

2. ___ ___

3. ___ ___

4. ___ ___

5. ___ ___

6. ___ ___

7. ___ ___

8. ___ ___

9. ___ ___

10. ___ ___

11. ___ ___

12. ___ ___

13. ___ ___

14. ___ ___

58

ra	ju
ve	va
ji	re
vi	jo
ro	vo
vu	je
ja	ru

2/2

1

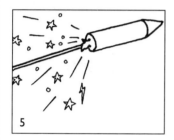

3

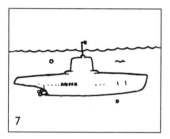

5

7

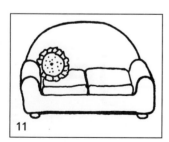

9

11

13

Write the first
2 letters
of these things.

1. ___ ___

2. ___ ___

3. ___ ___

4. ___ ___

5. ___ ___

6. ___ ___

7. ___ ___

8. ___ ___

9. ___ ___

10. ___ ___

11. ___ ___

12. ___ ___

13. ___ ___

14. ___ ___

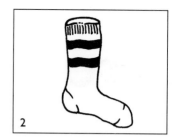

2

4

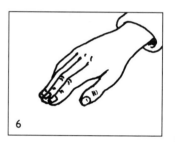

6

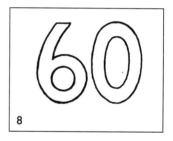

8

10

12

14

so

he

(2/3)

ri

sa

ha

ro

si

su

ru

ho

hu

se

re

ra

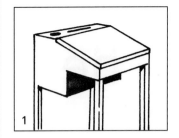

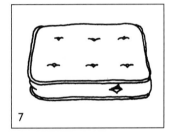

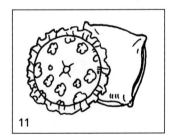

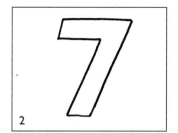

Write the first
2 letters
of these things.

1. __ __

2. __ __

3. __ __

4. __ __

5. __ __

6. __ __

7. __ __

8. __ __

9. __ __

10. __ __

11. __ __

12. __ __

13. __ __

14. __ __

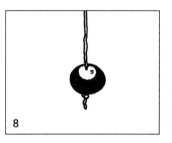

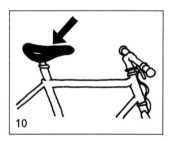

(2/4)

se	de
ca	mo
da	su
co	ma
sa	do
du	cu
mi	di

Write the first **2 letters** of these things.

1. __ __

2. __ __

3. __ __

4. __ __

5. __ __

6. __ __

7. __ __

8. __ __

9. __ __

10. __ __

11. __ __

12. __ __

13. __ __

14. __ __

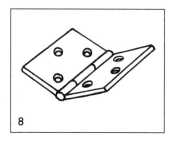

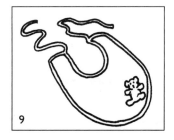

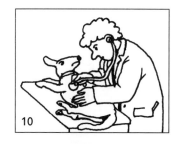

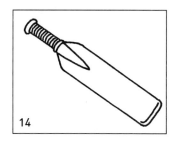

bu

vi

(2/5)

je

he

ta

bo

hi

ja

ve

bi

to

ha

ba

ju

1

2

3

4

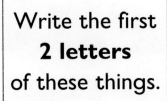

5

6

7

8

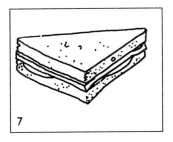

9

10

11

12

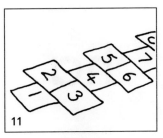

13

14

2/6

Write the first
2 letters
of these things.

1. ___ ___

2. ___ ___

3. ___ ___

4. ___ ___

5. ___ ___

6. ___ ___

7. ___ ___

8. ___ ___

9. ___ ___

10. ___ ___

11. ___ ___

12. ___ ___

13. ___ ___

14. ___ ___

de

go

(2/6)

he

ca

ga

do

je

sa

co

ro

ra

ho

ju

fa

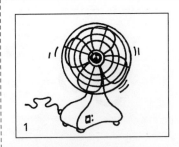

1

2

3

4

5

6

7

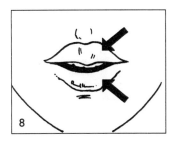

8

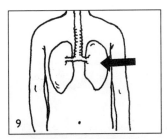

9

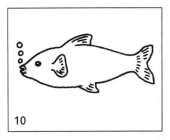

10

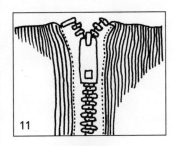

11

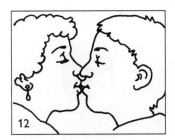

12

13

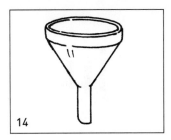

14

3/1

Write the first **2 letters** of these things.

1. ___ ___

2. ___ ___

3. ___ ___

4. ___ ___

5. ___ ___

6. ___ ___

7. ___ ___

8. ___ ___

9. ___ ___

10. ___ ___

11. ___ ___

12. ___ ___

13. ___ ___

14. ___ ___

ze

fa

(3/1)

le

ke

fe

la

li

fo

fi

lu

ki

zi

fu

lo

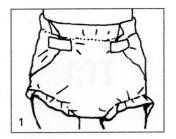

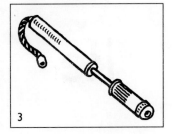

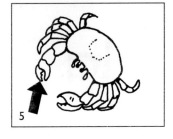

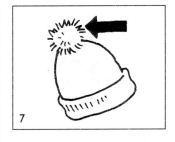

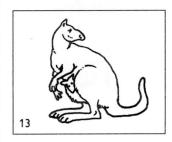

(3/2)

Write the first **2 letters** of these things.

1. ___ ___
2. ___ ___
3. ___ ___
4. ___ ___
5. ___ ___
6. ___ ___
7. ___ ___
8. ___ ___
9. ___ ___
10. ___ ___
11. ___ ___
12. ___ ___
13. ___ ___
14. ___ ___

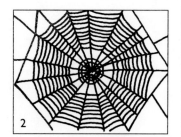

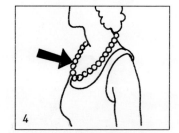

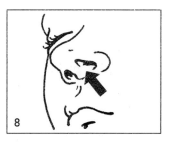

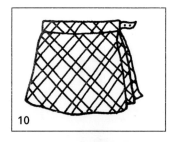

(3/2)

we	na
ne	pu
pa	ni
no	po
ki	nu
wi	pi
pe	ka

1

2

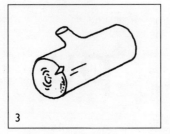

3

4

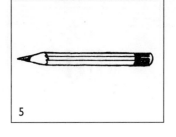

5

6

7

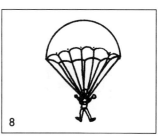

8

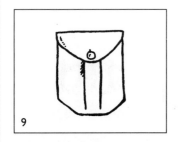

9

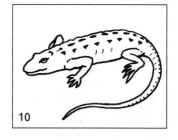

10

11

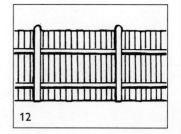

12

13

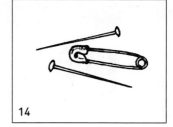

14

3/3

Write the first
2 letters
of these things.

1. __ __

2. __ __

3. __ __

4. __ __

5. __ __

6. __ __

7. __ __

8. __ __

9. __ __

10. __ __

11. __ __

12. __ __

13. __ __

14. __ __

pu	wi
fa	lo
we	pe
pa	la
li	po
fe	le
pi	fi

(3/3)

1

3

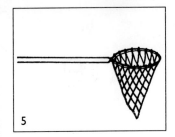

5

7

9

11

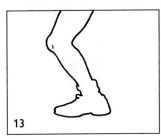

13

3/4

Write the first **2 letters** of these things.

1. ___ ___

2. ___ ___

3. ___ ___

4. ___ ___

5. ___ ___

6. ___ ___

7. ___ ___

8. ___ ___

9. ___ ___

10. ___ ___

11. ___ ___

12. ___ ___

13. ___ ___

14. ___ ___

2

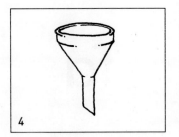

4

6

8

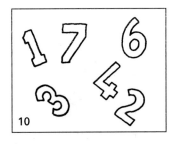

10

12

14

lo

pu

fu

la

pe

ne

li

fe

nu

pa

po

fi

pi

le

(3/4)

1

2

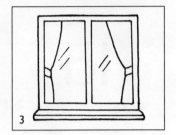

3

4

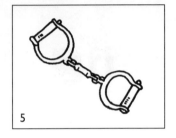

5

6

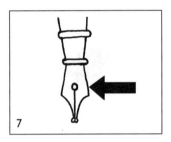

7

8

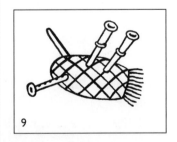

9

10

11

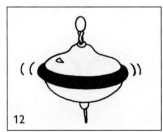

12

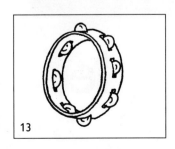

13

14

3/5

Write the first **2 letters** of these things.

1. ___ ___

2. ___ ___

3. ___ ___

4. ___ ___

5. ___ ___

6. ___ ___

7. ___ ___

8. ___ ___

9. ___ ___

10. ___ ___

11. ___ ___

12. ___ ___

13. ___ ___

14. ___ ___

he	ne
ke	wi
bo	ha
ka	ni
nu	ba
to	ki
bu	ta

(3/5)

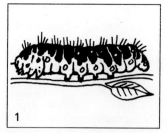

1

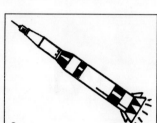

3

5

7

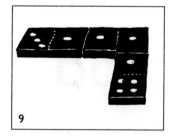

9

11

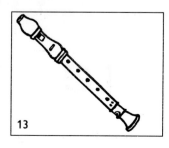

13

3/6

Write the first
2 letters
of these things.

1. __ __

2. __ __

3. __ __

4. __ __

5. __ __

6. __ __

7. __ __

8. __ __

9. __ __

10. __ __

11. __ __

12. __ __

13. __ __

14. __ __

2

4

$$3 +$$
$$4$$
___

6

8

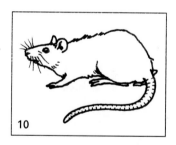

10

12

14

gu	3/6	ca
co		ro
su		cu
de		go
ra		do
du		sa
se		re

 3/7

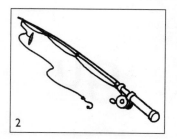

Write the first
2 letters
of these things.

1. __ __ __

2. __ __ __

3. __ __

4. __ __ __

5. __ __ __

6. __ __ __

7. __ __ __

8. __ __ __

9. __ __ __

10. __ __ __

11. __ __ __

12. __ __ __

13. __ __ __

14. __ __ __

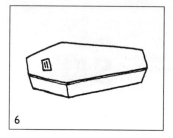

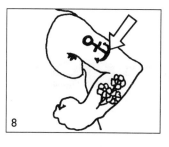

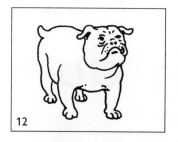

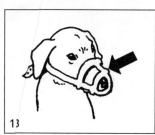

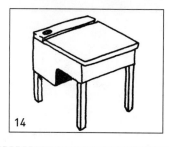

(3/7)

Ro	Ca
Hi	Ba
Co	Ma
Ta	Do
Ra	Ha
Bu	Te
De	Mu

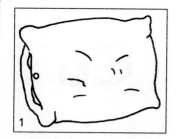

1

3

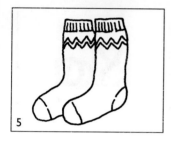

5

7

9

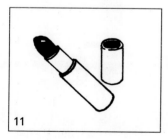

11

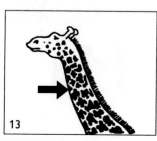

13

(3/8)

Write the first
2 letters
of these things.

1. __ __

2. __ __

3. __ __

4. __ __

5. __ __

6. __ __

7. __ __

8. __ __

9. __ __

10. __ __

11. __ __

12. __ __

13. __ __

14. __ __

2

4

6

8

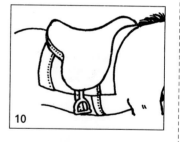

10

12

14

Ki

Nu

Pe

Lo

Sa

Va

Wi

3/8

Pi

Ve

So

Ke

We

Li

Ne

1

3

5

7

9

11

13

Write the first
2 letters
of these things.

1. ___ ___

2. ___ ___

3. ___ ___

4. ___ ___

5. ___ ___

6. ___ ___

7. ___ ___

8. ___ ___

9. ___ ___

10. ___ ___

11. ___ ___

12. ___ ___

13. ___ ___

14. ___ ___

2

4

6

8

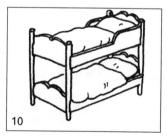

10

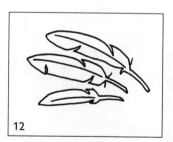

12

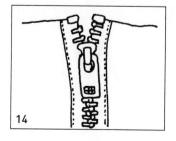

14

(3/9)

Do	Gu
Ju	Ba
Le	Fi
Ga	Ze
Bu	Je
Fe	Lo
Zi	Du

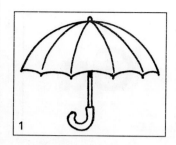

1

3/10

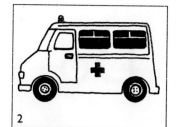

2

3

4

Write the first
2 letters
of these things.

1. __ __

2. __ __

3. __ __

4. __ __

5. __ __

6. __ __

7. __ __

8. __ __

9. __ __

10. __ __

11. __ __

12. __ __

13. __ __

14. __ __

5

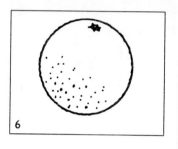

6

7

8

9

10

11

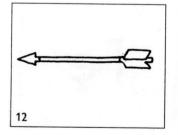

12

13

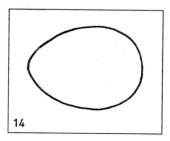

14

(3/10)

Am	Um
El	Ig
Or	Ap
In	Oc
Up	An
Ar	Un
Eg	Os

1

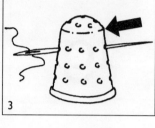

3

5

7

9

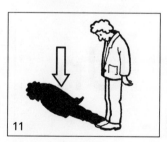

11

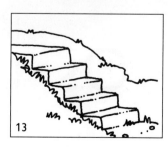

13

4/1

Write the first **3 letters** of these things.

1. _ _ _ _

2. _ _ _ _

3. _ _ _ _

4. _ _ _ _

5. _ _ _ _

6. _ _ _ _

7. _ _ _ _

8. _ _ _ _

9. _ _ _ _

10. _ _ _ _

11. _ _ _ _

12. _ _ _ _

13. _ _ _ _

14. _ _ _ _

2

4

6

8

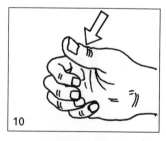

10

12

14

(4/1)

shi	cha
sta	thi
chi	she
sho	sto
thu	che
cho	sha
shu	ste

1

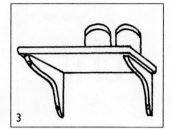

3

5

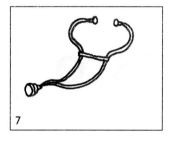

7

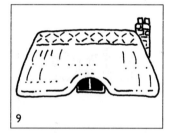

9

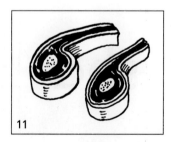

11

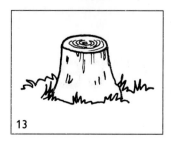

13

4/2

Write the first
3 letters
of these things.

1. ___ ___ ___

2. ___ ___ ___

3. ___ ___ ___

4. ___ ___ ___

5. ___ ___ ___

6. ___ ___ ___

7. ___ ___ ___

8. ___ ___ ___

9. ___ ___ ___

10. ___ ___ ___

11. ___ ___ ___

12. ___ ___ ___

13. ___ ___ ___

14. ___ ___ ___

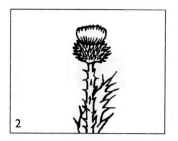

2

4

6

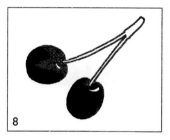

8

10

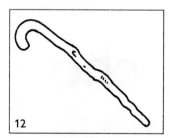

12

14

(4/2)

thi	sta
chi	she
sto	cha
che	ste
sho	tha
sti	cho
shu	stu

1

2

4/3

Write the first **3 letters** of these things.

3

4

1. ___ ___ ___

2. ___ ___ ___

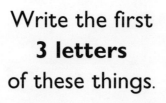

5

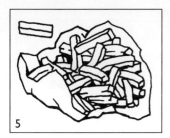

6

3. ___ ___ ___

4. ___ ___ ___

7

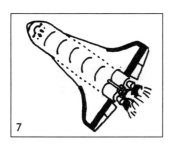

8

5. ___ ___ ___

6. ___ ___ ___

9

10

7. ___ ___ ___

8. ___ ___ ___

9. ___ ___ ___

11

12

10. ___ ___ ___

11. ___ ___ ___

12. ___ ___ ___

13

13

14

13. ___ ___ ___

14. ___ ___ ___

(4/3)

qui	sti
cha	sho
sto	chi
ste	shu
shi	che
que	sta
stu	she

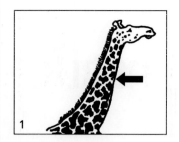

1

4/4

2

3

4

Write the words

1. _____

2. _____

3. _____

4. _____

5. _____

6. _____

7. _____

8. _____

9. _____

10. _____

11. _____

12. _____

13. _____

14. _____

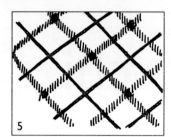

5

6

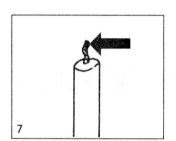

7

8

9

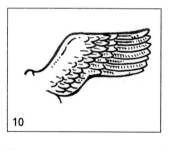

10

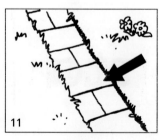

11

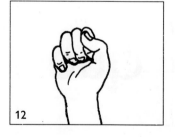

12

13

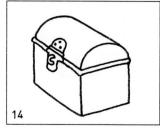

14

bath

pack

ring

nest

wing

fist

chest

(4/4)

neck

fish

check

wick

back

path

rich

1

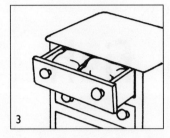

3

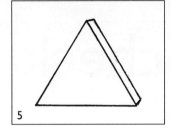

5

7

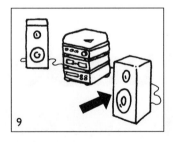

9

11

13

(5/1)

Write the first
2 letters
of these things.

1. __ __

2. __ __

3. __ __

4. __ __

5. __ __

6. __ __

7. __ __

8. __ __

9. __ __

10. __ __

11. __ __

12. __ __

13. __ __

14. __ __

2

4

6

8

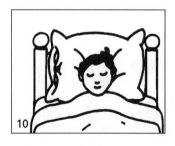

10

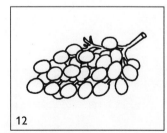

12

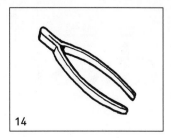

14

fl	(5/1)	sk
cr		dr
sm		tr
fr		gl
sl		sp
gr		br
tw		sw

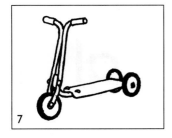

(5/2)

Write the first **2 letters** of these things.

1. __ __

2. __ __

3. __ __

4. __ __

5. __ __

6. __ __

7. __ __

8. __ __

9. __ __

10. __ __

11. __ __

12. __ __

13. __ __

14. __ __

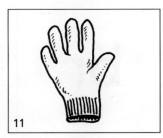

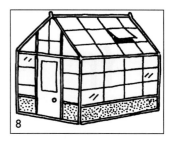

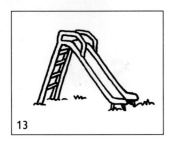

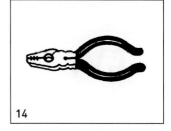

(5/2)

sn	bl
fr	pr
tr	cl
gr	sc
br	fl
cr	gl
pl	sl

1

3

5

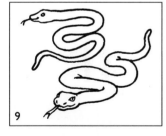

7

9

11

13

(5/3)

Write the first **2 letters** of these things.

1. ___ ___

2. ___ ___

3. ___ ___

4. ___ ___

5. ___ ___

6. ___ ___

7. ___ ___

8. ___ ___

9. ___ ___

10. ___ ___

11. ___ ___

12. ___ ___

13. ___ ___

14. ___ ___

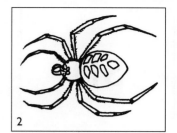

2

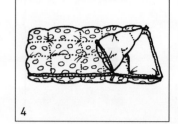

4

6

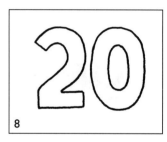

8

10

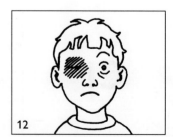

12

14

(5/3)

sp	fl
sl	gl
sw	pl
tw	sk
pr	sn
bl	gr
sm	br

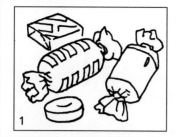

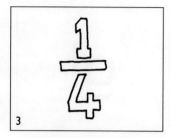

(5/4)

Write the first **2 letters** of these things.

1. _ _ _

2. _ _ _

3. _ _ _

4. _ _ _

5. _ _ _

6. _ _ _

7. _ _ _

8. _ _ _

9. _ _ _

10. _ _ _

11. _ _ _

12. _ _ _

13. _ _ _

14. _ _ _

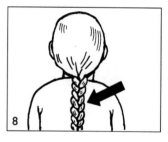

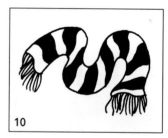

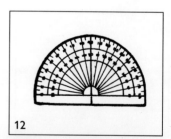

sh	(5/4)	sw
cl		qu
th		sn
pl		ch
sc		sm
pr		sp
st		fr

1

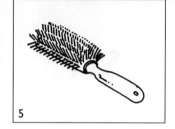

3

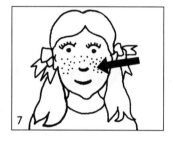

5

7

9

11

13

5/5

Write the first
2 letters
of these things.

1. __ __

2. __ __

3. __ __

4. __ __

5. __ __

6. __ __

7. __ __

8. __ __

9. __ __

10. __ __

11. __ __

12. __ __

13. __ __

14. __ __

2

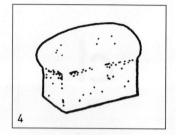

4

6

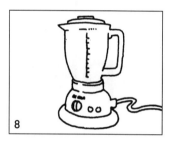

8

10

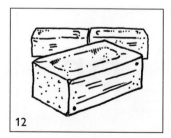

12

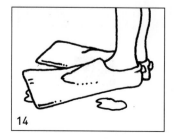

14

fri

bre

fra

ble

bli

bri

fli

(5/5)

fla

bla

bru

fre

bra

fro

blo

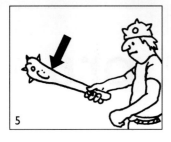

(5/6)

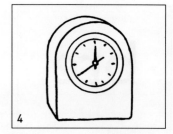

Write the first **3 letters** of these things.

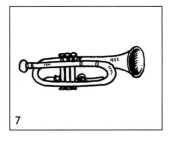

1. __ __ __

2. __ __ __

3. __ __ __

4. __ __ __

5. __ __ __

6. __ __ __

7. __ __ __

8. __ __ __

9. __ __ __

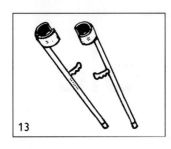

10. __ __ __

11. __ __ __

12. __ __ __

13. __ __ __

14. __ __ __

tre

cli

clo

tra

cri

clu

cla

tru

tri

tro

swe

swi

cro

cru

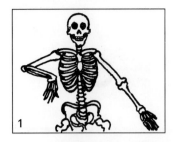

1

3

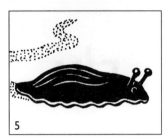

5

7

9

11

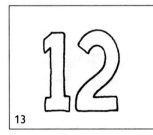

13

2

4

6

8

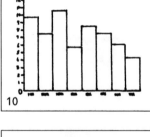

10

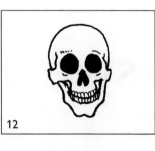

12

14

(5/7)

Write the first **3 letters** of these things.

1. ___ ___ ___

2. ___ ___ ___

3. ___ ___ ___

4. ___ ___ ___

5. ___ ___ ___

6. ___ ___ ___

7. ___ ___ ___

8. ___ ___ ___

9. ___ ___ ___

10. ___ ___ ___

11. ___ ___ ___

12. ___ ___ ___

13. ___ ___ ___

14. ___ ___ ___

5/7

sli	ske
sta	gru
sto	slu
twi	gla
gra	sle
sku	gri
gle	twe

1

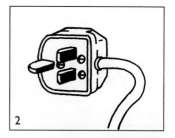

2

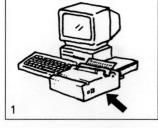

3

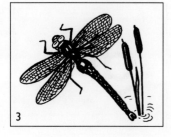

4

5/8

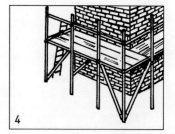

4

5

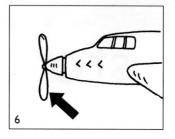

6

7

8

9

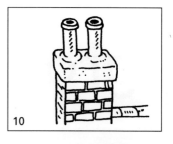

10

11

12

13

14

Write the first 3 letters of these things.

1. __ __ __
2. __ __ __
3. __ __ __
4. __ __ __
5. __ __ __
6. __ __ __
7. __ __ __
8. __ __ __
9. __ __ __
10. __ __ __
11. __ __ __
12. __ __ __
13. __ __ __
14. __ __ __

plu

(5/8)

pri

sca

dra

pro

pla

dre

Sco

chi

pre

pra

dri

dru

cho

(5/9)

Write the first **3 letters** of these things.

1. ___ ___ ___

2. ___ ___ ___

3. ___ ___ ___

4. ___ ___ ___

5. ___ ___ ___

6. ___ ___ ___

7. ___ ___ ___

8. ___ ___ ___

9. ___ ___ ___

10. ___ ___ ___

11. ___ ___ ___

12. ___ ___ ___

13. ___ ___ ___

14. ___ ___ ___

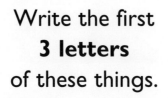

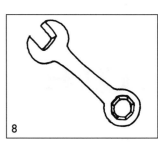

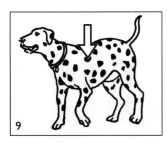

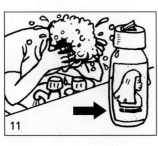

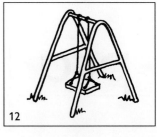

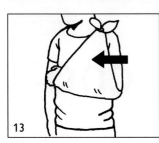

(5/9)

Sco	spi
sti	sta
stu	she
spa	sle
sme	spo
swi	sha
sho	sli

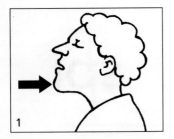

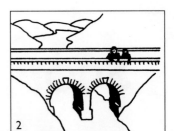

(5/10)

Write the first
3 letters
of these things.

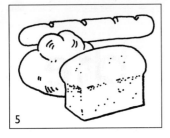

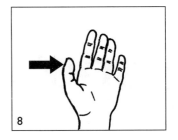

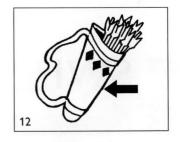

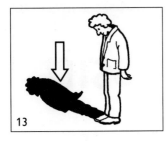

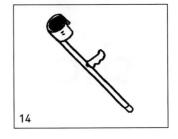

1. ___ ___ ___

2. ___ ___ ___

3. ___ ___ ___

4. ___ ___ ___

5. ___ ___ ___

6. ___ ___ ___

7. ___ ___ ___

8. ___ ___ ___

9. ___ ___ ___

10. ___ ___ ___

11. ___ ___ ___

12. ___ ___ ___

13. ___ ___ ___

14. ___ ___ ___

bri	chi
cho	que
shi	bre
thu	che
bru	cra
qui	thi
cru	sha

(5/10)

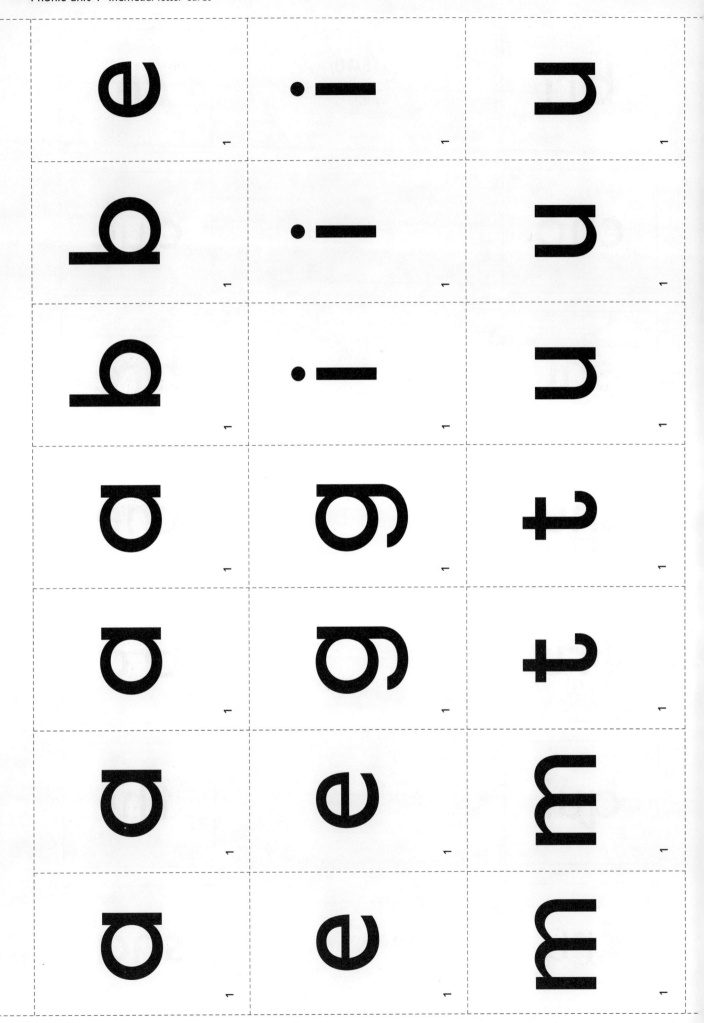

h
2

r
2

v
2

h
2

o
2

v
2

d
2

o
2

s
2

d
2

o
2

s
2

d
2

o
2

s
2

c
2

j
2

r
2

c
2

j
2

r
2

l	p	z
l	p	z
k	p	z
k	n	y
f	n	y
f	n	w
f	l	w

G

N

V

F

M

U

E

L

T

D

K

S

C

J

R

B

I

P

A

H

O

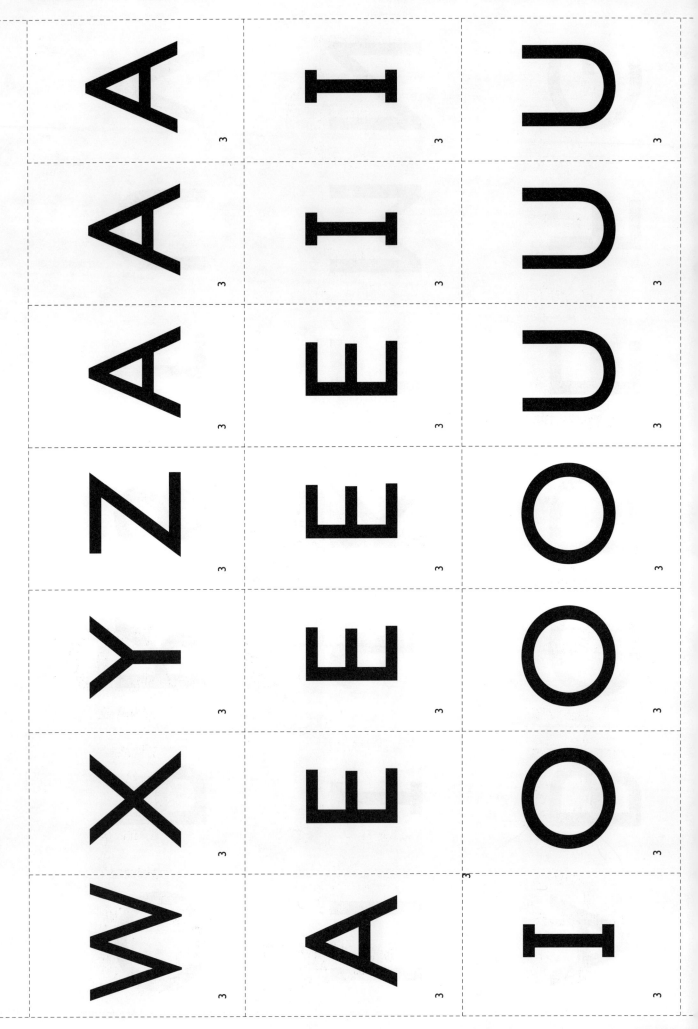

A A A
I I
U U U

Z E E
O O

Y E E
O O

W X E E
I

A

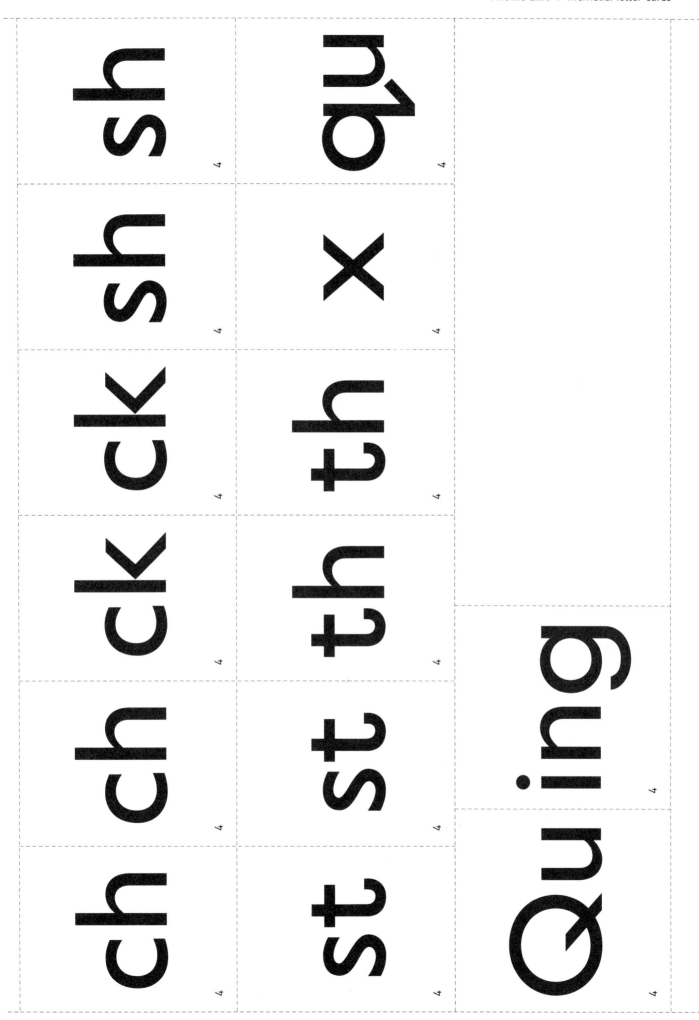

sh sh

ck ck

ch ch

qu

x

th th

st st

Qu ing

dr cr cl

br bl

pr pl

gr gl

fr fl

w

5

tr

sp

sn

sl

sk

sc

tw

sw

sm

5

5

5

5

5

5

5

5

mp

5

tch

5

nd

5

lf

5

lp

5

pt

5

ld

5

lm

5

nt

5

ft

5

lk

5

nk

5

ct

5

1		2			
am	tag	bad	dug	jig	sad
at	tig	bed	gas	job	sag
bag	tub	bid	god	jog	sat
bat	tug	bog	got	jot	set
beg		bud	had	jug	sit
bet		cab	ham	mad	sob
bib		cat	has	mob	sum
big		cod	hat	mud	tot
bit		cog	hem	rag	vet
bug		cot	hid	ram	vim
but		cub	him	rat	
gag		cut	his	red	
get		dab	hit	rib	
gig		dad	hob	rid	
gum		dam	hot	rig	
gut		did	hug	rim	
it		dig	hum	rob	
mat		dim	hut	rod	
met		dog	jab	rot	
mug		dot	jam	rub	
mum		dud	jet	rug	

3

an	hip	nap	pit	wet
ban	hop	net	pop	wig
bin	if	nib	pot	win
bun	in	nil	pup	yes
can	keg	nip	ran	yet
cap	kit	nod	rap	zip
cup	lad	not	rip	
den	lap	nun	run	
dip	led	nut	sap	
fan	leg	on	sip	
fat	let	pad	sun	
fed	lid	pal	tan	
fib	lip	pan	tap	
fin	lit	pat	ten	
fit	log	peg	tip	
fog	lot	pen	top	
fun	man	pet	up	
gap	map	pig	van	
gun	men	pin	wag	
hen	mop	pip	web	

4

ch	ck		qu	sh	st		th	x	ing	combinations
chat	back	rock	quin	shed	stab	just	than	box	ding	check
chin	deck	sack	quip	shin	stag	last	that	fix	king	chest
chip	dock	sick	quit	ship	step	list	them	fox	ping	chick
chop	duck	sock	quiz	shop	stop	lost	then	mix	ring	quack
chug	jack	suck		shot	stub	mast	thin	six	sing	quest
chum	kick	tack		shut	stud	mist	this	tax	wing	quick
much	lick	tick		ash	best	must	thud	wax		shack
rich	lock	tuck		bash	bust	nest	bath			shock
such	luck	wick		cash	cast	past	moth			stack
	muck			dash	cost	pest	path			stash
	neck			dish	dust	rest	with			sting
	pack			fish	fast	rust				stock
	peck			hush	fist	test				stuck
	pick			mash	gust	vest				thick
	rack			posh	jest	west				thing
				rash						

5

initial blends

black	clock	drum	glum	skip	snob	trod
blast	clog	flan	grab	slab	snug	trot
bled	clot	flap	grin	slack	span	truck
blip	cloth	flat	grip	slam	speck	trust
block	club	fleck	grit	slap	spin	twig
blot	cluck	flick	grub	slash	spot	twin
blush	crab	fling	plan	slid	spun	twist
brag	crack	flip	plot	slim	swam	
bran	crag	flit	plug	sling	swim	
brat	cram	flock	plum	slip	swing	
brick	crash	flush	plus	slog	swish	
brim	crest	fresh	pram	slug	swop	
bring	crib	fret	prod	slush	swot	
broth	crop	frog	prop	smack	swum	
brush	crush	frock	scab	smash	track	
clan	crust	from	scan	smock	trap	
clap	drag	frost	scat	smog	trash	
clash	drat	froth	scum	snack	trek	
click	drip	glad	skid	snag	trick	
cling	drop	glen	skim	snap	trim	
clip	drug	glug	skin	snip	trip	

5

final blends

act	kiln	fund	bent
fact	gulp	hand	hunt
daft	help	land	mint
gift	yelp	lend	sent
left	belt	mend	tent
lift	felt	pond	went
loft	kilt	sand	jinx
raft	melt	send	kept
soft	tilt	wind	wept
bulb	bump	bank	disc
held	camp	bunk	desk
weld	dump	honk	disk
elf	hump	junk	dusk
golf	jump	link	mask
self	lamp	pink	risk
bulk	limp	rink	rusk
hulk	lump	sink	tusk
milk	pump	tank	gasp
silk	ramp	wink	wisp
sulk	band	yank	next
film	bend	ant	text

initial and final blends

blank	drift	slept
blend	drink	smelt
blink	flash	spelt
blond	flint	spend
blunt	frisk	spent
brand	gland	spilt
brink	glint	stamp
champ	grand	stand
chimp	grant	stump
chump	grunt	stunt
chunk	plank	swank
clamp	plant	swept
clank	prank	swift
clink	primp	thank
clump	scalp	think
craft	scamp	thump
cramp	shelf	track
crept	shift	tramp
crisp	skint	trunk
croft	skunk	
drank	slant	

5

double letters

add	chill	shell	cross	
odd	doll	skill	dress	
biff	drill	skull	fuss	
bluff	dull	smell	glass	
cliff	dwell	spell	grass	
cuff	fell	spill	hiss	
duff	fill	still	kiss	
gruff	frill	swell	less	
huff	full	tell	loss	
off	grill	till	mass	
puff	gull	well	mess	
quiff	hill	will	miss	
scoff	ill	yell	moss	
sniff	kill	inn	pass	
staff	mill	bless	press	
stiff	pill	boss	nett	
stuff	pull	brass	putt	
egg	quill	chess	buzz	
bell	sell	class	fizz	
bill	shall	cress	jazz	

–tch

batch
blotch
catch
ditch
fetch
hatch
hitch
hutch
itch
match
patch
pitch
scotch
sketch
snatch
stitch
switch
twitch
witch

triple blends

scrap	squint
scratch	strap
script	stretch
scrub	strict
scruff	string
scrum	strip
shred	struck
shrill	thrash
shrimp	thresh
shrink	thrift
shrub	thrill
shrug	thrush
shrunk	
splash	
splat	
split	
spring	
sprint	
squib	
squid	

This is good!	Very good!	Very good!	Very good!
This is good!	Tip-top!	Tip-top!	Tip-top!
This is good!	Smashing!	Smashing!	Smashing!
This is good!	Splendid!	Splendid!	Splendid!
	Fantastic!	Fantastic!	Fantastic!
	Brilliant!	Brilliant!	Brilliant!

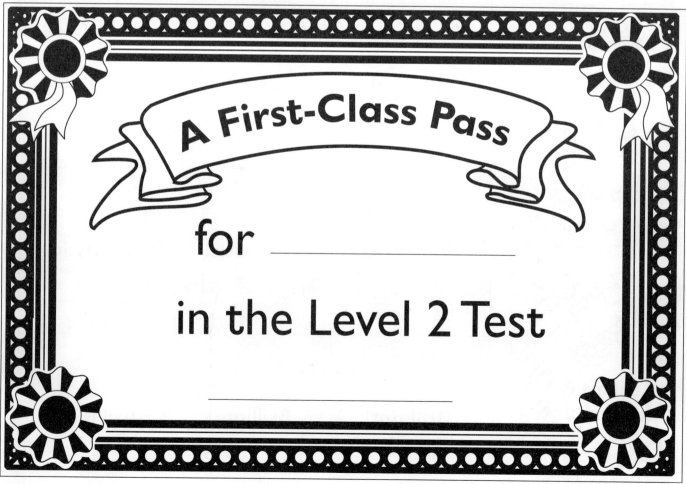

DAILY RECORD SHEET

Name	

Date Level 2 started				
Date Level 2 completed				

	Sequence of work	Started			Finished			Comments
		d	m	y	d	m	y	
CORE BOOKS	Word bank 7: 25 words (*words 2* pp. 3-9)							
	Book 7: *The glen*							
	Phonic unit 1: (*letters I* pp. 3-21)							
	Word bank 8: 25 words (*words 2* pp. 10-17)							
	Book 8: *The clan*							
	Phonic unit 2: (*letters I* pp. 22-41)							
	Wordbank 9: 25 words (*words 2* pp. 18-23)							
	Book 9: *The haggis hunt*							
	Phonic unit 3: (*letters I* pp.42-64)							
	Word bank 10: 25 words (*words 2* pp. 24-29)							
	Book 10: *Jock the pocket*							
	Phonic unit 4: (*Letters 2* pp. 3-25)							
	Word bank 11: 25 words (*words 2* pp. 30-35)							
	Book 11: *Don the bonnet*							
	Phonic unit 5: (*Letters 2* pp. 26-49)							
	Word bank 12: 25 words (*words 2* pp.36-43)							
	Book 12: *The contest*							
	Phonic unit 6: (*Letters 2* pp. 50-64)							
EXTENSION BOOKS	Extra Workbook: *More words and letters*							
	Book 12.1: *The slinx has a problem*							
	Book 12.2: *The biggest dump in the land*							
	Book 12.3: *The rocket*							
	Book 12.4: *Zaxon*							
	Book 12.5: *The Honkbonk*							
	Book 12.6: *Going back*							
	Book 12.7: *The gull*							
	Book 12.8: *The map*							
	Book 12.9: *The band*							
	Book 12.10: *The raft*							
	Book 12.11: *The depths*							
	Book 12.12: *The chest*							

TEST 1

creeps	house	she	orange
first	good	chief	river
without	because	all	slippery
goes	read	summer	crossbar
apple	grumpy	there	down
going	he	ready	bagpipes
sleep	comes	words	very
boots	happy	go	more
green	every	onto	something
play	coming	under	write

j	f	a	p	v	l	h

r	i	c	w	d	u	z

x	o	m	t	y	b	k

g	n	s	q	e

F	D	T	A	H	W	O

I	X	C	J	L	U	M

P	Y	B	K	R	E	Q

Z	G	N	S	V

TEST 3

dig	hum	job	kit	tax	van
cup	fat	yes	lip	run	wag
ship	thud	peck	quit	ring	chop
last	dish	bath	sting	quest	rich
trap	skin	plum	spot	twig	flat
slip	brag	drip	from	crop	grin
hand	milk	tank	desk	yelp	limp
raft	went	melt	jinx	disk	self
swift	spelt	clamp	grand	trunk	slept
squid	press	stitch	scruff	jazz	string
chill	scraps	switch	swell	shrink	stretch

boxing	lipstick	insect	traffic
crossing	chestnut	handstand	comic
lollipop	minibus	catapult	magnetic

The thrush

This is a thrush.

Its back and wings are brown.

It has a yellowish-brown chest, with lots of
black spots.

Thrushes often come into gardens.

They hop and run across the grass, hunting
for something to eat.

These are two of the things that thrushes eat:

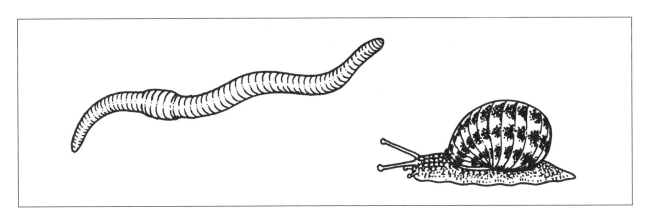

TEST 4(B)

Can you see an animal that lives in a shell?

It is difficult to eat this animal, so the thrush has a trick to get it out of its shell.

It picks up the shell in its bill, then hits it on a rock.

The shell smashes and the thrush can eat its dinner!

Often, the thrush picks just one rock to do this.

In spring, the hen thrush collects lots of grass and moss for her nest.

Thrushes' eggs are blue, with black spots.

The hen thrush sits on the eggs until they hatch into little chicks, called nestlings.

Now the hen and cock thrush must collect lots of insects for the chicks to eat.

Squirrels love to eat the little nestlings.

So if a squirrel gets into the tree where the nest is, the hen and the cock will attack it.

They will not give up until the squirrel runs off.

They will not let it get to the chicks.

Can you do these?
Do not forget full stops and capital letters.

1. Why do thrushes come into gardens?

2. How does the thrush get an animal out of its shell?

3. Why does the hen collect grass and moss?

4. What animal loves to eat nestlings?

5. Can you think of a pet animal that will attempt to get the nestlings?

6. Check what colour thrushes' eggs are, then pick the correct colours and colour this egg.

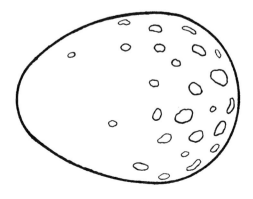

TESTS 1 & 2: RECORD SHEET

| Name | | | | | | | Date/s | | | | | | | | | |

creeps	house	she	orange
first	good	chief	river
without	because	all	slippery
goes	read	summer	crossbar
apple	grumpy	there	down
going	he	ready	bagpipes
sleep	comes	words	very
boots	happy	go	more
green	every	onto	something
play	coming	under	write

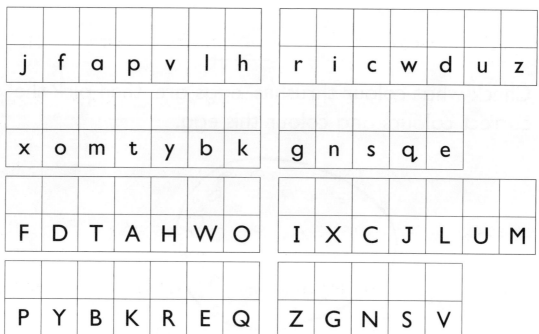

j	f	a	p	v	l	h

r	i	c	w	d	u	z

x	o	m	t	y	b	k

g	n	s	q	e

F	D	T	A	H	W	O

I	X	C	J	L	U	M

P	Y	B	K	R	E	Q

Z	G	N	S	V

fuzzbuzz Level 2

TEST 3: RECORD SHEET

| Name | | | Date/s | | | | | | | | |

1 dig hum job kit tax van

cup fat yes lip run wag

2 ship thud peck quit ring chop

last dish bath sting quest rich

3 trap skin plum spot twig flat

slip brag drip from crop grin

4 hand milk tank desk yelp limp

raft went melt jinx disk self

5 swift spelt clamp grand trunk slept

squid press stitch scruff jazz string

chill scraps switch swell shrink stretch

6 boxing lipstick insect traffic

crossing chestnut handstand comic

lollipop minibus catapult magnetic

© OUP: this may be reproduced for class use solely within the purchaser's school or college

TEST 4: RECORD SHEET 1

Name		Date/s								

The thrush

This is a thrush. Its back and wings are brown. It has a yellowish-brown

chest, with lots of black spots. Thrushes often come into gardens. They

hop and run across the grass, hunting for something to eat. These are

two of the things that thrushes eat. Can you see an animal that lives in a

shell? It is difficult to eat this animal, so the thrush has a trick to get it

out of its shell. It picks up the shell in its bill, then hits it on a rock. The

shell smashes and the thrush can eat its dinner! Often, the thrush picks

just one rock to do this. In spring, the hen thrush collects lots of grass and

moss for her nest. Thrushes' eggs are blue, with black spots. The hen

thrush sits on the eggs until they hatch into little chicks, called nestlings.

Now the hen and cock thrush must collect lots of insects for the chicks to

eat. Squirrels love to eat the little nestlings. So if a squirrel gets into the

tree where the nest is, the hen and the cock will attack it. They will not

give up until the squirrel runs off. They will not let it get to the chicks.

Name		Date/s									

Can you do these?
Do not forget full stops and capital letters.

1. Why do thrushes come into gardens?

_____

_____

2. How does the thrush get an animal out of its shell?

_____

_____

3. Why does the hen collect grass and moss?

_____

_____

4. What animal loves to eat nestlings?

_____

5. Can you think of a pet animal that will attempt to get the nestlings?

_____

6. Check what colour thrushes' eggs are, then pick the correct colours and colour this egg.

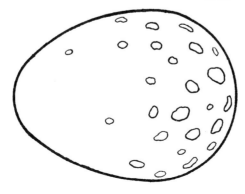

TEST SUMMARY SHEET

| Name | | Date/s | | | | | | | | | |

Test	**Task**	
1	Can read a selection of sight words from Levels 1 and 2	☐
2	Can vocalise the sounds of the lower-case letters when presented in random order	☐
2	Can vocalise the sounds of the upper-case letters when presented in random order	☐
3 ①	Can read regular three-letter words (c-v-c)	☐
3 ②	Can read one-syllable words containing ch, ck, ing, qu, sh, st, th	☐
3 ③	Can read four-letter words with initial consonant blends	☐
3 ④	Can read four-letter words with final consonant blends	☐
3 ⑤	Can read one-syllable words with initial and final blends	☐
	Can read one-syllable words with final double letters (e.g. ff, ll)	☐
	Can read one-syllable words with initial triple-consonant blends	☐
3 ⑥	Can read regular words of two and three syllables	☐
4	Can read, and answer written questions on, a piece of continuous prose based on all the skills outlined above	☐